LANGUAGE!®
The Comprehensive Literacy Curriculum

PLACEMENT
LANGUAGE READING SCALE

TEACHER EDITION

Jane Fell Greene, Ed.D.

Sopris West®

Sopris West®
EDUCATIONAL SERVICES

A Cambium Learning Company

BOSTON, MA • LONGMONT, CO

Copyright 2009 (Fourth Edition) by Sopris West Educational Services.
All rights reserved.

7   8   HPS   14   13   12   11

Authors:
Jane Fell Greene, Ed.D.
Nancy Chapel Eberhardt

MetaMetrics, Lexile, Lexile Framework and the Lexile symbol are trademarks or U.S. registered trademarks of MetaMetrics, Inc. The names of other companies and products mentioned herein may be the trademarks of their respective owners.
© 2006 MetaMetrics, Inc.

No portion of this work may be reproduced or transmitted by any means, electronic or mechanical, including photocopying or recording, or by any information storage and retrieval system, without the express written permission of the publisher.

ISBN 13 digit: 978-1-60218-675-0
ISBN 10 digit: 1-60218-675-8

169199/3-11

Printed in the United States of America

Published and distributed by

Sopris West®
EDUCATIONAL SERVICES

A Cambium Learning® Company

4093 Specialty Place • Longmont, CO 80504 • (303) 651-2829
www.sopriswest.com

Table of Contents

The *LANGUAGE!* Reading Scale (LRS) Placement Test
Placement Test Features 5
Description 6

Administration and Scoring Procedures
Basic Administration Procedures 7
Specific Administration Instructions.. 8
Scoring the LRS Tests 11
Interpreting the LRS Results 11
Recording of LRS Scores... 11
Test Scores and Their Interpretation 12

Using Test Scores for Placement Decisions
Placement Decisions for Students in Grades 3 through 12........ 15
Review and Acceleration... 16
Summary of the Placement Process 16
Communicate with Parents Meaningfully.................................. 16

LRS Scoring Keys
LRS Scoring Key for Placement Test for Grades 3 through 5..... 17
LRS Scoring Key for Placement Test for Grades 6 through 12 .. 18

LRS Answer Forms and Conversion Charts
LRS Student Answer Form—Placement 19
LRS Student Answer Form Key—Placement Grades 3–5 20
LRS Student Answer Form Key—Placement Grades 6–12......... 21
Converting LRS Placement Test Raw Scores to Lexile® Measures 22
Placement Class Roster... 24

Overview

The *LANGUAGE!* Reading Scale (LRS) Placement Test

Purpose

The *LANGUAGE!* Reading Scale (LRS) Placement Test is a group-administered assessment that helps to determine the appropriate instructional placement for students into book level A, C, or E.

The LRS Placement Test is intended for students who score below the 40th percentile on group-administered standardized tests used by districts and states to monitor reading progress. Based on their test performance, students can begin the curriculum at one of three main entry points:

Book A
For students demonstrating a deficiency in basic decoding and reading at roughly grades pre-primer to 2.5.

Book C
For students showing proficiency with beginning sound-symbol correspondences but deficiencies at higher levels of word analysis and reading at roughly grades 3–5.

Book E
For students in grades 7–12 who show proficiency with sound-symbol correspondences and higher levels of word analysis but are reading two or more years below grade level.

Placement Test Features

The LRS Placement Test measures students' reading comprehension skills. Specifically, it measures the ability to construct meaning while reading a passage. The test is not intended to provide an exhaustive assessment of literacy, but rather to serve as a valid measure of students' reading comprehension skills. Reading comprehension performance is related to skill levels in other literacy areas such as fluency, grammar and writing.

There are two grade-span versions of the *LANGUAGE! Reading Scale Placement Test*, each in a separate student booklet:

- *LANGUAGE! Reading Scale Placement Test*, Grades 3–5, student booklet
- *LANGUAGE! Reading Scale Placement Test*, Grades 6–12, student booklet

The appropriate placement test should be used depending on the grade level of the student being tested.

Placement

Description

The LRS Placement Test was developed using the Lexile® Framework for Reading. The Lexile Framework for Reading is a normed measurement system that measures reading comprehension. This means that the LRS Placement Test results can be linked to the Lexile national norms to measure how well readers comprehend expository text.

The *LRS Placement Test* has the following features:

- Consists of seven nonfiction passages on a variety of topics; the passages are arranged in order of increasing text difficulty.

- Test items are formed by the deletion of words from the passages. For each missing word, four possible words are provided. Students are asked to select the best word to fill in the blank.

- When considered in the context of the sentence with the word deletion, each word choice is plausible, both semantically and syntactically. When the missing word is considered within the context of the surrounding text, however, only one response is correct. Thus, responding correctly requires understanding (i.e., comprehending) the text surrounding the word. The words do not draw on background knowledge but depend on information in the passage; all information needed to answer correctly is provided in the passage.

- Yields a raw score and percentile rank. The test also reports a Lexile measure that represents a students' current reading ability in terms of the most difficult text in Lexile® measures that the students can comprehend with assistance from teachers or parents.

- Is group-administered, untimed and can be completed within one 50-minute class period.

The student's results are reported as a Lexile measure. The Lexile Framework for Reading provides teachers and educators with tools to help them link assessment results with subsequent instruction. Assessments such as those in *LANGUAGE!* that are linked to the Lexile scale provide tools for monitoring the progress of students at any time during the course. Readers interested in additional information about the Lexile Framework for Reading and its correlation to many other well-established tests of reading comprehension should see the *LANGUAGE! Reading Scale Technical Guide* found at www.teachlanguage.com.

Administration and Scoring Procedures

This section explains how to administer and score the LRS. The discussion includes (a) basic administration procedures, (b) specific administration instructions, and (c) scoring the LRS.

Basic Administration Procedures

The examiner can assure a reliable administration of the test by adhering to the following simple rules:

1. Comply with local school policies and state regulations, regarding test administration, interpretation, and issues of confidentiality.
2. If a student has a 504 plan or an Individualized Education Plan that calls for accommodations in a testing situation, make sure to implement the appropriate accommodations.
3. Provide an environment conducive to test taking including a quiet room, good lighting, appropriate furniture and writing tools.
4. Promote test-taking readiness by encouraging students to be well-rested and motivated.
5. Review the specific directions for administration and scoring provided for the *LRS Placement Test* prior to the testing session.
6. Deliver the instructions for the test verbatim.
7. Repeat the instructions as many times as needed.
8. Students should not practice the test or study the words or passages in the test either before or after the tests are administered.
9. The test should not be used for teaching purposes; do not correct students' errors.
10. Allow about 50 minutes for students to complete the test. Each test administration should take place in one class period.
11. Keep the test in a secure place. Distribute the booklets immediately before testing, and collect them as soon as a testing session is done.
12. Encourage students to do their best.

This test can be administered to entire classes, to small groups, or to individual students (e.g., to a student receiving remedial instruction or to a special education student). The same instructions are used for all forms.

Placement

Specific Administration Instructions

The following administration instructions apply when administering the LRS Placement Test. The same instructions are used for both test levels: grades 3–5, and grades 6–12.

To administer the LRS, each student will need two sharpened No. 2 pencils.

Step 1:

Distribute one LANGUAGE! Reading Scale Placement *booklet to each student. Have students turn to page 1. Check to see that students are on the correct page.*

Step 2:

SAY:

- **Do not turn the page until I tell you to.**

Once all students have opened to the correct page, continue below.

SAY:

- **Find where it says "Directions to the Student"** *(point).* **Read silently while I read out loud.**

Hold up a test booklet to show the students the correct page. Check that all students have opened their booklets to the correct page. When everyone has found the page:

SAY:

- **Today you will take the** *LANGUAGE! Reading Scale Test.* **This reading test contains passages for you to read. Words are missing from the passages. Where a word is missing, there is a blank line with a number on it. Next to the passage on the right side, you will find the same number and four words. These are the answer choices. Read each sentence carefully, and then choose the best word to complete the sentence based on what you have read. Next to the word you will fill in the bubble for the answer you have chosen.**

SAY:

- **Find the paragraph for Sample S-1. It is inside the box labeled SAMPLE.**

Teachers should not read the sample items out loud. They are printed here only for the teacher's information.

Providing practice with standardized test-taking procedures

One way to provide students an opportunity to practice standardized test-taking procedures is to have them record their answers onto a student answer form. A reproducible Student Answer Form and a corresponding scoring key can be found on pages 19-21. If you want to use the Student Answer Form, distribute one to each student and ask them to write their names and the date on the form before reading the directions.

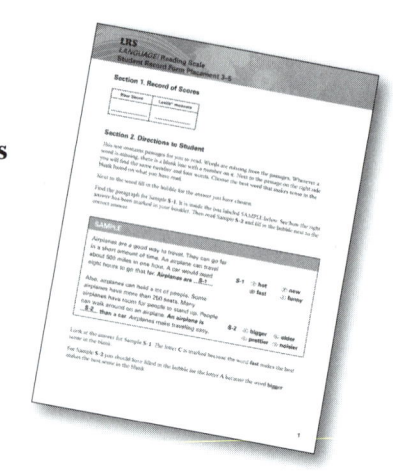

Administration and Scoring Procedures

> **SAMPLE**
>
> Airplanes are a good way to travel. They can go far in a short amount of time. An airplane can travel about 500 miles in one hour. A car would need eight hours to go that far. **Airplanes are __S-1__**.
>
> S-1   Ⓐ hot   Ⓑ new
>   Ⓒ fast   Ⓓ funny
>
> Also, airplanes can hold a lot of people. Some airplanes have more than 250 seats. Many airplanes have room for people to stand up. People can walk around on an airplane. **An airplane is __S-2__ than a car**. Airplanes make traveling easy.
>
> S-2   Ⓐ bigger   Ⓑ older
>   Ⓒ prettier   Ⓓ noisier

Next, hold up the test booklet to point to the paragraph below the word "Sample 1." When everyone has found the paragraph:

SAY:

- Read the paragraph for Sample S-1.

*If students are using **a separate answer form**, then hold up an answer sheet and point to the words "SAMPLE ITEMS." When everyone has found the section:*

SAY:

- On your answer sheet, find the answer for Sample S-1. The bubble for the letter "C" is filled in because the word "fast" makes the best sense in the blank.
- Now do Sample S-2 on your own.

Give students time to complete Sample S-2 by themselves. Then proceed to Step 3 below.

<u>Step 3:</u>

SAY:

- On your answer sheet, find the same number as the blank. Fill in the bubble next to the answer you have chosen for Sample S-2. Remember to completely fill in the circle corresponding to the answer you choose.

*If students are using **the test booklet**:*

SAY:

- Look at the answer for Sample S-1. The bubble for the letter "C" is filled in because the word "fast" makes the best sense in the blank.
- Now do Sample S-2 on your own.

Give students time to complete Sample S-2 by themselves. Then proceed to Step 3 below.

<u>Step 3:</u>

SAY:

- Fill in the bubble next to the answer you have chosen for Sample S-2. Remember to completely fill in the circle corresponding to the answer you choose.

Placement

Step 4:

After students have completed Sample S-2:

SAY:

- For Sample S-2 you should have filled in the bubble for the letter "A" because the word "bigger" makes the best sense in the blank.

Assist students who do not understand the instructions. When everyone is ready:

SAY:

- Now turn your test booklet to the next page. Look at the rest of the directions. Read them silently while I read them out loud. Before you begin working in your test booklet, here are a few reminders:
    - Try to complete as many of the test items as you can.
    - There is no time limit, so do not hurry to complete the test.
    - Be sure to choose the best answer based on the information in the passage.
    - Remember to mark only one answer choice for each item.
    - Check all of your answers after completing the test.
    - When you are finished with your test, please place your answer sheet inside of the test booklet. Close the test booklet and put it in the corner of your desk. You may then take out a book and read silently until further notice.

*If students are using **a separate answer form**, then:*	*If students are using **the test booklet**, then:*
Hold up a Student Answer Form and point to Question 1. When everyone has found Question 1 on their answer sheet,	*Hold up the test booklet and point to Question 1. When everyone has found Question 1 in their test booklet:*
SAY:	SAY:
• This is where you will mark your answer to Question 1. Now turn your test booklet to Question 1. You may now begin working in your booklet.	• Now turn your test booklet to Question 1. This is where you will mark your answer to Question 1. You may now begin working in your booklet.

Administration and Scoring Procedures

After students have begun the test:

- *Check to make sure that each student is following the directions.*
- *You may help individual students, as long as assistance is limited to mechanical aspects of marking answers and clarifying directions. DO NOT do the following:*
    - *Indicate a correct answer*
    - *Tell students words in the passage*
    - *Provide clues for answering an item.*
- *If a student is marking answers without reading test items, encourage the student to study each item carefully.*

After students have done all they can:

- *Tell students to stop and collect all student answer forms and student LRS Placement booklets.*

Scoring the LRS Tests

Score the test using the answer key on page 20 for grades 3–5 and page 21 for grades 6–12 of this booklet.

The raw score is the total number of items answered correctly.

Interpreting the LRS Results

This section presents information about interpreting the LRS results.

The topics to be addressed include (a) how to record the scores, (b) how to interpret the scores, and (c) using student test results for placement decisions.

Recording of LRS Scores

Converting raw scores to Lexile® measures can happen in two ways: manually or by using the *Online Assessment System*. The *Online Assessment System* provides users with Lexiles, percentiles and placement recommendations. Without use of the *Online Assessment System* (manual recording of scores), only Lexiles are provided.

Online Assessment System	Manual
Converts raw scores to: • Lexile® measures • percentile ranks Uses test results to make placement recommendations. **Note:** There is no need to use print record forms	Converts raw scores to: • Lexile® measures **Note:** Must use placement criteria on page 15 and the following print record forms: LRS Placement Student Record Form, Placement Class Roster.

11

Placement

Recording Using the *LANGUAGE! Online Assessment System*

Enter raw scores into the *LANGUAGE! Online Assessment System*. The Web-based data entry and reporting system will convert raw scores to Lexile® measures and percentiles, and use the test results to make placement recommendations.

Detailed discussions of the Lexile measures and percentile ranks are found in the "Test Scores and Their Interpretation" section of this chapter.

Manual Recording

Use the conversion table on page 22 to convert the LRS raw scores to Lexile measures. For example: A raw score of 30 on the test for grades 6–12 converts to a Lexile measure of 595 (595L). A detailed discussion of Lexile measures is found in the next section.

Once Lexiles are obtained, scores should be recorded on the print record forms:

- **LRS Placement Student Record Form**—An individual's placement test performance is recorded on the LRS Student Record Form on page 19.
- **Placement Class Roster**—This form records all placement scores for a class. Transfer scores from the students' LRS Placement Record Forms to the Placement Class Roster found on page 24.

Test Scores and Their Interpretation

The chart below shows the scores provided for the LRS: raw scores, Lexile measures, and percentile ranks. This section includes a brief discussion of each score and how it should be interpreted. The shortcomings of these scores and cautions about their use are also discussed.

| Scores Provided ||
Online Assessment System	Manual
Converts raw scores to: • Lexile® measures • percentile ranks	Converts raw scores to: • Lexile® measures

Raw Scores

A student's raw score on the test is the number of items the student answered correctly. For example, if a student correctly answered 16 items on the 49-item test, his or her raw score would be 16. These scores are only useful for generating Lexile® scores and percentile ranks.

Administration and Scoring Procedures

Lexile® Measures

A **Lexile® reader measure** represents a student's reading ability on the Lexile scale. The Lexile scale is a scale for reporting reading ability, so a higher number represents a higher level of reading ability. A Lexile reader measure is reported in intervals of 5L (Lexile), from a low of 5L to a high of 2000L. Readers who score at or below a reported level of 5L receive a score of BR (Beginning Reader). A student's score on the *LANGUAGE! Reading Scale* is reported as a Lexile reader measure.

> Raw scores are converted to Lexile reader measures using the *LANGUAGE! Online Assessment System* or the table on page 22.

A **Lexile® text measure** represents a text's difficulty level on the Lexile scale. A Lexile text measure, like a Lexile reader measure, is reported on the Lexile scale. A Lexile text measure is reported in intervals of 10L, from a low of 10L to a high of 2000L. The lower a book's Lexile measure, the easier it will likely be to comprehend. For example, a text with a Lexile measure of 850L will most likely be easier for a reader to comprehend than a text at 950L. A Lexile text measure of 10L or below is reported as BR, which means that the text is appropriate for a Beginning Reader. The text selections within *LANGUAGE!* have been rated on the Lexile text measure scale.

The **Lexile® reader measure** and the **Lexile® text measure** can be used together to predict how well a student will likely comprehend a text at a specific Lexile level. For example, if a student has a Lexile measure of 1000L, she will be forecasted to comprehend approximately 75 percent of a book with the same Lexile measure (1000L). When the Lexile measure and the Lexile scale were developed, the 75-percent comprehension rate was set as the point where the difference between the Lexile reader measure and the Lexile text measure is 0L. The 75-percent comprehension rate is called "targeted" reading. This rate is based on independent reading; if the student receives assistance, the comprehension rate will increase. The target reading rate is the point at which a student will comprehend enough to understand the text, but will also face some reading challenge. At this challenge point, a reader is not bored by text that is too easy, but also does not experience too much difficulty in understanding.

When a student takes the *LRS Placement Test*, his or her results are reported as a Lexile measure. This means, for example, that a student whose reading ability has been measured at 500L is expected to read with 75-percent comprehension a book that is also measured at 500L. When the reader and text are matched (same Lexile measures), the reader is "targeted." A targeted reader reports confidence, competence, and control over the text. When a text measure is 250L above the reader's measure, comprehension is predicted to drop to 50 percent and the reader will likely experience frustration and inadequacy. Conversely, when a text measure is 250L below the reader's measure, comprehension is predicted to go up to 90% and the reader is expected to experience control and fluency. When reading a book within his or her Lexile range (50L above his or her Lexile measure to 100L below), the reader is forecasted to comprehend enough of the text to make sense of it, while still being challenged enough to maintain interest and learning.

Placement

Percentile Ranks

Percentile ranks indicate the percentage of the distribution that is equal to or below a particular score. For example, a percentile rank of 30 means that 30% of the norming sample scored at or below the student's score, and 70% of the norming sample scored above the student's score. The norming sample for the Lexile Framework® for Reading included a nationally-representative sample of students. Because this interpretation is easy to understand, percentile ranks are often used by practitioners when sharing test results with others. The distance between two percentile ranks increases as they move farther from the mean or average (i.e., the 50th percentile). Therefore, percentile ranks cannot be arithmetically manipulated (e.g., by adding, subtracting, or averaging the scores) in the same manner as Lexile scores. Although percentile ranks are convenient and popular, examiners should be familiar with their advantages and disadvantages as explained by Aiken (2000)[1], McLoughlin and Lewis (2001)[2], and Salvia and Ysseldyke (2001)[3].

> Raw scores are converted to percentile ranks using the *LANGUAGE! Online Assessment System.*

[1]Aiken, L. R. (2000). *Psychological testing and assessment* (8th ed.). Needham Heights, MA: Allyn & Bacon.

[2]McLoughlin, J. A., & Lewis, R. B. (2001). *Assessing students with special needs* (5th ed.). Upper Saddle River, NJ: Merrill/Prentice Hall.

[3]Salvia, J., & Ysseldyke, J. E. (2001). *Assessment* (8th ed.). Boston: Houghton-Mifflin.

Placement Decisions

Using Test Scores for Placement Decisions

Once the test is administered and scored and the test information is recorded in the Placement Class Roster, teachers use decision criteria—in combination with teacher judgment based on student needs—for placing students at one of the three entry points in the curriculum:

- Book A, Unit 1
- Book C, Unit 13
- Book E, Unit 19

When students do not meet the criteria for placement in Book A, Book C, or Book E, then they may be considered for Review and Acceleration instruction in the curriculum and/or placement in the core reading program.

In addition to the results of the placement tests, teacher judgment based on students' needs should contribute to placement decisions. Use writing samples and other pertinent assessments, including tests of reading and language skills, to assess students' learning needs.

Placement Decisions for Students in Grades 3 Through 12

Use the *LRS Placement Test* Lexile® scores to determine placement level.

Grade Level	Lexile	Placement Recommendation
Grade 3	Below 430L	Book A
	Above 430L	Core Reading Program
Grade 4	Below 430L	Book A
	430L – 575L	Book A, Review and Acceleration*
	Above 575L	Core Reading Program
Grade 5	Below 430	Book A
	430L – 700L	Book C
	Above 700L	Core Reading Program
Grade 6	Below 430L	Book A
	430L – 800L	Book C
	Above 800L	Core Reading Program
Grades 7 - 12	Below 430L	Book A
	430L – 800L	Book C
	800L – 950L	Book E
	Above 950L	Core Reading Program

Placement

*Review and Acceleration

Students who score in the upper end of the placement range for their grade level should place in the curriculum but can move at a faster pace. The teacher should use the Review and Acceleration path, identified by the starred activities on each unit Lesson Planner page, in Books A and B Teacher Editions to provide accelerated coverage of instruction.

Summary of the Placement Process

1. Administer the test.
2. Obtain a raw score for the *LRS Placement Test* by using the Scoring Key provided in this booklet.
3. **If using the *Online Assessment System*—**Enter raw scores in the *Online Assessment System* to automatically convert raw scores to Lexile® measures, percentile ranks and placement recommendations.
4. **If recording scores manually—**Convert raw scores to Lexiles using the table on page 22. Record scores on the Placement Class Roster. Compare each student's Lexile measure to the placement criteria on page 15 to generate placement recommendations.

Communicate with Parents Meaningfully

Teachers can use the LRS data to provide specific information about their child's reading comprehension status. For example, a teacher might say: "Your child will be able to read with at least 75% comprehension these kinds of materials which are at the next grade level." Or, "Your child will need to be able to increase his/her Lexile measure by 400-500 Lexiles in the next few years to be prepared for college reading demands. Here is a list of appropriate titles your child can choose from for reading this summer."

LRS Scoring Key

LRS Scoring Key for Placement Test for Grades 3–5

1. a	22. c	43. a
2. c	23. b	44. d
3. c	24. a	45. d
4. d	25. d	46. c
5. c	26. b	47. b
6. b	27. b	48. d
7. b	28. d	49. a
8. a	29. c	
9. d	30. a	
10. a	31. b	
11. b	32. d	
12. a	33. a	
13. b	34. c	
14. c	35. d	
15. d	36. b	
16. b	37. a	
17. c	38. c	
18. c	39. a	
19. a	40. c	
20. a	41. a	
21. a	42. b	

Placement

LRS Scoring Key for Placement Test for Grades 6–12

1. b	22. b	43. b
2. b	23. c	44. c
3. a	24. d	45. c
4. d	25. d	46. a
5. c	26. b	47. a
6. b	27. c	48. d
7. a	28. a	49. c
8. c	29. b	
9. d	30. a	
10. a	31. d	
11. a	32. b	
12. b	33. a	
13. c	34. a	
14. c	35. c	
15. b	36. a	
16. d	37. d	
17. a	38. a	
18. d	39. d	
19. c	40. b	
20. a	41. a	
21. b	42. a	

LRS Student Answer Form

Name _____ Date _____

LRS Student Answer Form—Placement

S-1 Ⓐ Ⓑ ● Ⓓ	S-2 Ⓐ Ⓑ Ⓒ Ⓓ	
1. Ⓐ Ⓑ Ⓒ Ⓓ	18. Ⓐ Ⓑ Ⓒ Ⓓ	35. Ⓐ Ⓑ Ⓒ Ⓓ
2. Ⓐ Ⓑ Ⓒ Ⓓ	19. Ⓐ Ⓑ Ⓒ Ⓓ	36. Ⓐ Ⓑ Ⓒ Ⓓ
3. Ⓐ Ⓑ Ⓒ Ⓓ	20. Ⓐ Ⓑ Ⓒ Ⓓ	37. Ⓐ Ⓑ Ⓒ Ⓓ
4. Ⓐ Ⓑ Ⓒ Ⓓ	21. Ⓐ Ⓑ Ⓒ Ⓓ	38. Ⓐ Ⓑ Ⓒ Ⓓ
5. Ⓐ Ⓑ Ⓒ Ⓓ	22. Ⓐ Ⓑ Ⓒ Ⓓ	39. Ⓐ Ⓑ Ⓒ Ⓓ
6. Ⓐ Ⓑ Ⓒ Ⓓ	23. Ⓐ Ⓑ Ⓒ Ⓓ	40. Ⓐ Ⓑ Ⓒ Ⓓ
7. Ⓐ Ⓑ Ⓒ Ⓓ	24. Ⓐ Ⓑ Ⓒ Ⓓ	41. Ⓐ Ⓑ Ⓒ Ⓓ
8. Ⓐ Ⓑ Ⓒ Ⓓ	25. Ⓐ Ⓑ Ⓒ Ⓓ	42. Ⓐ Ⓑ Ⓒ Ⓓ
9. Ⓐ Ⓑ Ⓒ Ⓓ	26. Ⓐ Ⓑ Ⓒ Ⓓ	43. Ⓐ Ⓑ Ⓒ Ⓓ
10. Ⓐ Ⓑ Ⓒ Ⓓ	27. Ⓐ Ⓑ Ⓒ Ⓓ	44. Ⓐ Ⓑ Ⓒ Ⓓ
11. Ⓐ Ⓑ Ⓒ Ⓓ	28. Ⓐ Ⓑ Ⓒ Ⓓ	45. Ⓐ Ⓑ Ⓒ Ⓓ
12. Ⓐ Ⓑ Ⓒ Ⓓ	29. Ⓐ Ⓑ Ⓒ Ⓓ	46. Ⓐ Ⓑ Ⓒ Ⓓ
13. Ⓐ Ⓑ Ⓒ Ⓓ	30. Ⓐ Ⓑ Ⓒ Ⓓ	47. Ⓐ Ⓑ Ⓒ Ⓓ
14. Ⓐ Ⓑ Ⓒ Ⓓ	31. Ⓐ Ⓑ Ⓒ Ⓓ	48. Ⓐ Ⓑ Ⓒ Ⓓ
15. Ⓐ Ⓑ Ⓒ Ⓓ	32. Ⓐ Ⓑ Ⓒ Ⓓ	49. Ⓐ Ⓑ Ⓒ Ⓓ
16. Ⓐ Ⓑ Ⓒ Ⓓ	33. Ⓐ Ⓑ Ⓒ Ⓓ	
17. Ⓐ Ⓑ Ⓒ Ⓓ	34. Ⓐ Ⓑ Ⓒ Ⓓ	

Placement

Photocopy this page on a transparency to make a LRS scoring overlay to use with the LRS student answer form.

LRS Student Answer Form Key—Placement Grades 3–5

S-1	S-2	
C	A	
1. A	18. C	35. D
2. C	19. A	36. B
3. C	20. A	37. A
4. D	21. A	38. C
5. C	22. C	39. A
6. B	23. B	40. C
7. B	24. A	41. A
8. A	25. D	42. B
9. D	26. B	43. A
10. A	27. B	44. D
11. B	28. D	45. D
12. A	29. C	46. C
13. B	30. A	47. B
14. C	31. B	48. D
15. D	32. D	49. A
16. B	33. A	
17. C	34. C	

LRS Student Answer Form Keys

Photocopy this page on a transparency to make a LRS scoring overlay to use with the LRS student answer form.

LRS Student Answer Form Key—Placement Grades 6–12

S-1 (C)	S-2 (A)	
1. B	18. D	35. C
2. B	19. C	36. A
3. A	20. A	37. D
4. D	21. B	38. A
5. C	22. B	39. D
6. B	23. C	40. B
7. A	24. D	41. A
8. C	25. C	42. A
9. D	26. B	43. B
10. A	27. C	44. C
11. A	28. A	45. C
12. B	29. B	46. A
13. C	30. A	47. A
14. C	31. D	48. D
15. B	32. B	49. C
16. D	33. A	
17. A	34. A	

21

Placement

Converting LRS Placement Test Grade 3–5 and Grades 6–12 Raw Scores to Lexile® Measures

Grades 3–5 Reported Lexile® Measure	Raw Score for All Grade Levels	Grades 6–12 Reported Lexile® Measure
BR	0	BR
BR	1	BR
BR	2	BR
BR	3	BR
BR	4	BR
BR	5	15L
BR	6	55L
BR	7	90L
BR	8	125L
BR	9	155L
BR	10	185L
BR	11	210L
BR	12	235L
BR	13	260L
BR	14	280L
10L	15	305L
30L	16	325L
50L	17	345L
65L	18	365L
85L	19	385L
105L	20	405L
120L	21	425L
140L	22	445L
155L	23	460L
175L	24	480L
190L	25	500L
210L	26	520L
225L	27	535L
245L	28	555L
260L	29	575L
280L	30	595L
300L	31	615L
320L	32	635L
335L	33	655L
355L	34	675L
375L	35	695L
400L	36	720L
420L	37	745L

(Continued on next page)

LRS Correspondence Tables

Grades 3–5 Reported Lexile® Measure	Raw Score for All Grade Levels	Grades 6–12 Reported Lexile® Measure
445L	38	770L
470L	39	795L
495L	40	820L
525L	41	850L
555L	42	885L
590L	43	920L
635L	44	965L
680L	45	1010L
740L	46	1075L
740L	47	1075L
740L	48	1075L
740L	49	1075L

Placement

Placement Class Roster

Student Name	Test Date (MM/DD/YY)	LRS Lexile® Measure	Placement Recommendation